Golf: How to CONSISTENTLY Break 90

Christian Henning & Robert Phillips

Golf: How to CONSISTENTLY Break 90
By Christian Henning & Robert Phillips

Published by IGD Publishing
2410 W. Memorial Road, Suite 332c
Oklahoma City, OK USA
405-640-1186

Table of Contents

My Gift to You

Thank you for purchasing this book. My hope is that you are able to lower your score and become more consistent. More importantly, I want you to enjoy the game of golf more than ever.

Apply the basic strategies in this book and you are sure to shave a few strokes off your scorecard.

Honestly, I wanted to give this book away for free.

Unfortunately, Amazon forces me to charge something for it. They do allow me to offer it free for five days out of a 90 day period though. So if you were lucky enough to snag it for free, congrats!

To give you a bit more bang for your buck, I have a free gift for you.

As my way of saying thanks for purchasing this book, I want to give you my Pre-round Warm Up. The warm up takes 15 minutes and gets your body, mind, and swing prepared for a round of golf.

Many of my clients have used this warm up all by itself to help lower their scores. The pre-round warm up is included with all of my golf fitness programs and I am very happy to offer it to you at no additional cost.

Go Here to Download => http://getgolffit.com/how-to-break-90-gift/

All you need to do is enter a valid email address and shortly after I will send you a link to download the full version of the Pre-round Warm Up.

Chris Henning

P.S. I would appreciate a positive review of the information provided in the book. I also would love to hear from you and how this book has helped you. Please email me at cs@getgolffit.com.

Chapter 1 :
The Breaking 90
Blueprint

How to Consistently **Break 90...**

A proven blueprint for breaking 90, not just once, but <u>every</u> time you tee it up!

Thank for downloading this valuable report. If you struggle to break 90 and you're *serious* about lowering your scores into the 80's consistently, then you're in the right place.

You see, not long ago, I was in your shoes. I would jump for joy when I shot 80-something. Unfortunately, more often than not, my final score was 90-something. It was frustrating. You can probably relate.

The GOOD NEWS is that I ultimately came up with systematic plan for breaking 90 on a consistent basis. These days, my score is usually in the low to mid-80s. And I've even broken 80 several times. The first time I shot 79 was really exciting!

But this is NOT about me. It's about YOU! You just need to know that I've walked the course in your shoes, shared your frustrations, and shattered the barrier you're about to break. And I want to help you break 90 every time you tee it up – and reach that level sooner rather than later.

According to the National Golf Foundation, fewer than 20% of golfers break 90 consistently. So when you apply the systematic approach laid out in this report and start shooting in the 80s regularly, you'll be in that elite group of 1 out of 5 golfers who consistently break 90.

And perhaps the best news is the requirements for joining the elite club of golfers consistently shooting in the 80's don't include spending hundreds or even thousands of dollars on new clubs. New clubs may (or may not) help, but if you can master a few basic skills, you can consistently break 90 with *any* set of golf clubs.

Before we get started, let me be clear. This report is NOT about the golf swing or the mechanics of the golf swing. It's not about putting or chipping. I have a few tips to share but if you're already shooting in the 90's, you're way past the point of hitting ground balls. You just need a proven blueprint to shave strokes of your score. And that's exactly what you'll discover in these pages.

This is a simple and systematic approach to breaking 90 on a regular basis – and while I encourage you to keep practicing and keep improving – you can probably break 90 with your current golf skills.

I'll share some thoughts that have helped me and suggest some resources you may find useful. But mostly what I'm going to do is share the simple system I've developed for breaking 90 consistently.

As you get better, you can fine tune this system to break 85 and then 80.

Let's Get Started!

If you're like me, you don't want long, drawn out, overly complicated explanations. You just want the proven blueprint – NOW!! So I'll give you the cliff notes version first and then get into more detail. Fair enough?

Here's the deal: On a par 72 course, if you bogey every hole, you'll shoot 90. So to break 90, all you have to do is par one hole – as long as you bogey the rest.

In other words, to break 90 consistently, you need to become just fractionally better than a "bogey golfer."

All you need to do is master a few simple, basic golf skills:

- ✓ Consistently hit your tee shots 200 yards or more AND keep it in play
- ✓ Consistently hit a reasonably straight iron shot (or hybrid) of 150 yards or more
- ✓ Consistently hit the green from 100 yards or less…
- ✓ And consistently 2-putt most greens…

That's it!! Just four simple things.

None of it is extraordinary. Those are just basic golf skills anyone of average strength and athleticism can master relatively quickly.

I wouldn't be surprised if you consistently hit your drives farther than 200 yards and if that's the case then you're ahead of the game (as long as you keep them in play!). Otherwise you'll probably lower your scores by throttling back a little and keeping your drives in play.

If you can't quite hit a consistent 150 yard iron shot (or hybrid if you prefer), then just work with what you have for now. And work toward the goal of consistently hitting a 150 yard shot (or even longer). I have several ideas to share on achieving this goal later in this report.

Consistently hitting the greens from 100 yards and in goes a long way toward shooting in the 80's. If that's your challenge, there's a simple system you can follow to zone in on the greens from 100 yards or less.

And finally the vital skill that often separates the low 90's golfer from the mid 80's golfer – putting. If putting is your nemesis, I'll explain how to minimize the dreaded three putts. If you can two-putt most greens, you're well on your way to breaking 90 consistently.

If you can already do all of those things and you're not consistently breaking 90, then you need a better strategy and I'll share it with you in this report.

I'll cover each of these skills later in this report. You can pick and choose what information you need or don't need. For example if you can already bomb your drives 250+ yards and split the middle of the fairway, but you struggle with your putting, then you can skip the section on hitting 200 yard drives and study the section on putting.

Fair enough?

Before you even tee it up...

First things first. Before you even tee it up for your first shot, it's important that you play from the appropriate tees. You may not like this (especially if you're a high-testosterone male like me!) but if you're going to break 90, you need to play from the tees appropriate to your skill level.

Think about it. If you're a snow skier, do you start on the double-black diamond trail? Only if you have a death wish! You'd be much better off starting on an easier trail – maybe even the "bunny hill" until your skill level improves to the point where you can ski harder trails.

[Note: If you're not familiar with snow skiing, the trails are usually marked to indicate their level of difficulty. The "bunny hill" is the easiest and that's where beginners should start. As your skill level improves you can move on to more difficult slopes that are steeper and have more obstacles like moguls or bumps.

It would be incredibly stupid for a beginner to start on a double-black diamond trail. Those are for accomplished skiers with very high skill levels. A beginner would risk serious injury attempting to ski down such a difficult slope.

So what does all of this have to do with golf?

And with you consistently breaking 90?

Plenty!!

Just as the beginner skier shouldn't attempt to ski down a difficult slope, a golfer who can't consistently break 90 should NOT be playing from the "double black diamond" tee boxes set up for scratch or single digit handicap golfers. It's a recipe for frustration, disaster, and triple-digit scores too!

Fortunately golf is not nearly as dangerous as snow skiing so you're not going to kill yourself playing from tee boxes too difficult for your skill level, but you will kill your chances of breaking 90 on a consistent basis.

Golf courses are set up to accommodate the wide variety of golfers with varying degrees of skill depending on what set of tees you play from. You can think of the obstacles on golf courses (like trees, water hazards, and sand traps) as being similar to moguls on a ski slope.

Playing the white tees (or the gold tees if you're a senior golfer or the red tees if you're female golfer) removes some of these obstacles. For example, fairway bunkers and water hazards that may be in play from the blue or black tees may be no problem at all from the white tees.

So if necessary, I recommend you swallow some pride and play from the tee boxes appropriate to your skill level.

OK, enough with my sermon. I'm not your father and I know you're going to play whatever tee boxes you want to play. All I ask is that you at least consider playing the white tees instead of the blue or black tees. Just try it once as a test and see for yourself how it lowers your scores.

Here's a typical scorecard with multiple sets of tees. Some scorecards will even indicate by handicap the skill level recommended for each set of tees but this one does not.

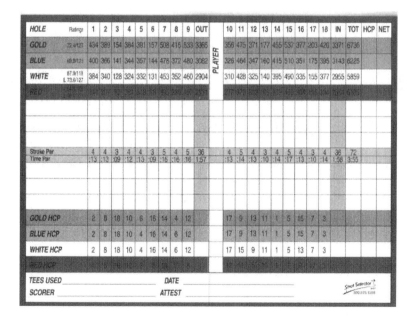

Each course could be set up slightly differently as far as the colors of the tee boxes but typically the back tees (in this case the gold tees) are for the best golfers – usually single digit handicaps who can break 80 consistently. You should NOT be playing these tees.

The next tees (the blues on this scorecard) are for mid-handicap golfers which would be something like 10 to 15. That means these golfers routinely break 90. And since you're not quite at that level yet, it's best to wait until you're breaking 90 consistently to play from these tees.

The white tees are for high handicap golfers. And if you're not consistently breaking 90 yet, then you are a high handicap golfer and you should be playing these tees – at least for now.

The total yardage should be around 6,000 yards total – maybe a bit more or maybe slightly less. In this case, the total yardage of the white tees is 5,859 yards. Perfect! At this distance, you should have a reasonable expectation of reaching the greens in regulation.

Some courses have tees especially for seniors. And of course the red tees are for female golfers.

You may be tempted to play the blue tees, but if you do you're only making it more difficult to break 90. You will significantly increase your chances of shooting a score in the 80s and having more fun if you tee it up from the white tees.

And that's the whole goal of this report: to provide you with a simple system for breaking 90 on a regular basis. As a matter of fact, it makes so much sense to "tee it forward" that the PGA and USGA launched a "tee it forward" initiative recently.

The program has been a success. Golfers who followed that advice and moved up to the next tee box reported they played faster, had more fun, and will continue to "tee it forward." And let's face it; golf is more fun when you shoot lower scores.

OK, let's move on. Now that you've chosen the set of tees that give you the best chance of breaking 90, let's talk about…

Your "Personal Par"…

As a starting point, take a look at each hole and figure out your "personal par." Par for the course is 72. That's obvious. But you aren't going to par every hole. So let's assign a score you can realistically expect to score on each hole.

There are several ways to do this:

You could just add a stroke to every hole. So every par 3 becomes a par 4, the par 4's are now par 5's, and each par 5 is now a par 6. It all adds up to 90.
And to break 90, all you have to do is shoot one better than that. Simple.

You can make adjustments according your skill level. For example, if you think you can reach all the par 3's, then your personal par on those holes is 3. And since now your personal par adds up to 86, you have a 3 stroke "cushion" to play with.

If you're a long hitter, you can make 5 your "personal par" on all the par 5's. It depends on your level of skill and confidence. Unfortunately, I can't make that decision for you.

But if you do need me to make that decision for you, here's a simple solution. Add one stroke to the par of every hole except the easiest hole on the course. Each hole is given a handicap that's shown on the card.

The #1 handicap hole is judged to be the hardest and the #18 handicap hole is judged to be the easiest. In this case, the #18 handicap hole is the third hole from the white tees.

Your "personal par" on hole #3 would be 3 and your "personal par" on every other hole is the regular par plus one.
So your scorecard now looks like this:

Hole	1	2	3	4	5	6	7	8	9	Out	10	11	12	13	14	15	16	17	18	In	Total
Par	4	4	3	4	4	3	5	4	5	36	4	5	4	3	4	5	4	3	4	36	72
Score	5	5	3	5	5	4	6	5	6	44	5	6	5	4	5	6	5	4	5	45	89

If you think you can par all the par 5's, then your scorecard would look like this:

Hole	1	2	3	4	5	6	7	8	9	Out	10	11	12	13	14	15	16	17	18	In	Total
Par	4	4	3	4	4	3	5	4	5	36	4	5	4	3	4	5	4	3	4	36	72
Score	5	5	4	5	5	4	5	5	5	43	5	5	5	4	5	5	5	4	5	43	86

You get the idea.

And now that you've got your "personal par" figured out for each hole and put it in writing, pat yourself on the back. Why? Because you now have a plan in place. You know what you need to score on every hole to break 90. Now it's time to execute your plan.

But let me be clear. Just because your "persona par" might be 5 when the regular par is 4, I'm not saying you need to play it as a 3 shot hole (meaning taking 3 shots to reach the green) and then two-putt for a 5 which is your "personal par."

Not at all!

It depends on your skill level (mostly your distance) and the length of the hole. Anyone ought to be able to reach a 350 yard hole in two shots. But as the holes get longer, they'll be harder to reach in two shots.

If you can hit a 230 yard drive and 170 yard second shot, then you can reach 400 yard par 4s and you should go for it. On the other hand, if you can hit 200 yard drives and 150 yard second shots, you should play it as a 3 shot hole. Leaving yourself a short pitch shot for your third shot will lead to lower scores than trying to play above your skill level.

But if you're not consistently breaking 90, then you're probably not hitting a lot of greens in regulations. That means you're often pitching or chipping to the green for your third shot. And you can still two-putt for your "personal par."

The extra shot is just a "cushion." If you don't need that cushion, then that's all the better. Sometimes you'll reach the green in regulation and two-putt for par. And that puts you on track to break 90.

So don't play defensively because your "personal par" is one stroke above regular par. But don't play too aggressively and try to reach long par 4s (or par 5s) in two shots when it's not realistic that you'll reach them. Play it smart, lay up, and leave yourself with an easy shot.

Let's move on...

Don't ruin your round before the 1st hole...

I shouldn't have to say this but before you hit your first tee shot, you will have at least stretched and stroked a few putts to get a feel for the speed of the greens that day. And it would be even better if you hit a few range balls – but I understand there's not always enough time for that. So at least stretch and stroke a few putts.

Going to the first tee cold is a recipe for disaster. How many times have you gotten off to a slow start on the first few holes and then started playing well when you got loose?

Plus getting double-bogeys (or worse) on the first couple holes certainly does not put you on the most positive mental state. Some golfers let getting off to a slow start ruin their entire round.

Don't let that happen to you. Warm-up before your round. Stretch, stroke some putts, and hit some range balls.

In fact, I've crafted an entire pre-round warm up from car trunk to tee box that gets you warmed up and mentally ready to play golf. This program includes:

✓ Warming Up the Body
✓ Warming Up the Mind for Lower Scores
✓ How to Warm Up Your Golf Swing
✓ How to Fine-tune Distance Control

The Pre-Round Warm Up gets a lot of positive reviews from my golf fitness clients:

"Used your pre-round warm-up... Saved 2-4 strokes over 9 holes!" – Richard H.

As my way of saying thanks for purchasing this book, I want to give you my

Pre-round Warm Up. The warm up takes 15 minutes and gets your body, mind, and swing prepared for a round of golf.

Many of my clients have used this warm up all by itself to help lower their scores. The pre-round warm up is included with all of my golf fitness programs and I am very happy to offer it to you at no additional cost.

Go Here to Download => http://getgolffit.com/how-to-break-90-gift/

All you need to do is enter a valid email address and shortly after I will send you a link to download the full version of the Pre-round Warm Up.

Play within yourself

Golfers get themselves in trouble when they play too aggressively. You don't need to be "hero" and hit 250 or 300 yards drives to break 90. You don't have to attack pins to break 90. All you need to do is execute the plan you've already written down on your scorecard.

Playing "within yourself" means accepting that you can consistently hit a 200 yard drive and keep it in play or a 225-yard drive and keep it in play. It also means you recognize that when you over swing and try to get an extra 25 yards out of your drive bad things happen. That's when your duck hook or slice suddenly reappears. That's when you put yourself in trouble and that's when your scores quickly soar above your "personal par." And if you keep pressing for the entire round, that's when your score skyrockets over 90.

Playing "within yourself" means hitting a 3-wood, 5-wood, or hybrid club off the tee because that's the club that keeps the ball in play. What's the point of hitting a 250-yard drive if it ends up in trouble most of the time? You'd be better off (and shoot lower scores) hitting a 3-wood 225 or a 5-wood 200 and keeping it in play.

When selecting an iron, take one more club if you have to. For example, instead of crushing your 8-iron or 9-iron 150, take a smooth swing with your 7-iron. You get the same score no matter what club you hit so play the "smart" club.

Just play "within yourself" and the desired results will follow.

Play smart

Like I said, you don't need to be overly aggressive to break 90, you just need to execute your plan. Shoot for the middle of the green, not for the pin on your approach shots.

When you get into trouble, as you occasionally will, get out of trouble with your next shot. Just put the ball back in play and go from there. Don't try to be a hero. Don't think you're Phil Mickelson if you can't break 90 consistently. Phil can pull off "miracle shots" but even Phil gets himself in more trouble when he doesn't execute the "hero shot."

And that's the problem. More often than not, instead of pulling off the great shot you envisioned, you screw it up and put yourself in an even worse spot.
Golf guru Dave Pelz has done extensive research that shows most golfers play below their handicap for most of their rounds. But they "blow up" on two or three holes and that's what explodes their scores. Playing "smart" may not eliminate "blow up" holes but it will reduce your chances of scoring a 7, 8, or higher on any single hole.

Play away from hazards like water and bunkers or sand traps. Think about it. If your "personal par" is a bogey, then all you need to do is get the ball near the green in two shots (or in three shots on a par 5). Then you just chip it on the green, two-putt and walk off the green with your "personal par" – one hole closer to breaking 90.

Playing "smart" and playing "within yourself" goes a long way toward keeping big numbers off your scorecard and ultimately shooting scores in the 80's.

Play One Hole at a Time...

You often hear athletes talk about playing one game at a time or playing one play at a time. What they mean is that they play a whole season in one game. Losing one game doesn't ruin the season. And messing up one play probably won't lose the game.

Taking this concept to golf, you can't break 90 in one hole. And just because you have one bad hole, doesn't mean you can't still break 90. You can score a stroke or two over your "personal par" on a hole and still break 90. Sure, it will be more challenging because you're going to have to make up those lost strokes but it can be done.

Don't lose faith because of one bad shot or one bad hole. Even professional golfers hit bad shots. They just recover and move on from those bad shots. And you should do the same. But there's a big difference between a professional and a high-handicapper.

PGA pros can not only get out of trouble but hit extraordinary recovery shots and hit greens from the most unlikely places. A player with less skill, like you, should look for the easiest way to get the ball back in play such that they still have a chance to score their "personal par" on the hole. Just punch it back into the fairway if that's all you've got.

Remain focused on the shot at hand. Don't get caught up in the negative emotions of one bad hole and don't look too far forward to the holes in front of you. Focus your energy and attention on the shot you're taking at the moment. But before you hit each shot think about the next shot. In other words…

Play the Hole Backwards…

You may find it helpful to play the hole backwards. All that means is think about your next shot and where you'd like to hit it from, then hit your current shot to that spot.

For example, let's say you're playing a 370-yard hole. It's a par 4 but your "personal par" is 5. And let's say you feel really comfortable hitting an 8-iron from 140 yards out. Knowing that, you need to hit a 230yard drive (370 yards less 230 yard drive leaves 140 yards to the pin).

Now let's say you hit your tee shot a bit "fat" so you hit it 215-yards and even push it a bit right (assuming you're a right-handed golfer) into the rough.
Let's also say the pin is tucked behind a bunker on the right side of an elevated green, there's another greenside bunker to the right, and if you go long you're out-of-bounds in the trees.

What do you do? The dumb play is to "attack" the pin. Unless you're a low-handicap golfer, you have no business even thinking about attacking that pin. That brings all kinds of bad things into play.

Instead of hitting a great shot and having a birdie putt, the more likely outcome – given that you're a high-handicap golfer – is that you're next shot will either be in the bunker or if you don't end up in the bunker, you'll be "short-sided" meaning you won't have much green to work with for your next shot making it difficult to chip it close.

Now you've brought a score of 6 or higher into play. Not smart!!

The "smart play is aim to the center or even left side of the green. Remember, your "personal par" is 5. If you put it on the green, you can three-putt and still score a 5 – your "personal par." Or even better, you could two-putt for a real par.

And if you're not on the green with your second shot, when you aim left of the pin to avoid trouble, you leave yourself a much easier chip shot with a lot more green to work with. It will be infinitely easier to chip the ball on the green and two-putt for your personal par than it would be to do the same thing from either the sand trap or from a "short-sided" lie.

By playing each hole backwards, you're actually thinking one shot ahead. And as you can clearly see that will save you strokes and help you break 90.

And that's the short story. Let's recap:

Step #1: Select the tees appropriate for your skill level to increase your chances of breaking 90. On most courses, these will be the white tees and the total yardage should be about 6,000 yards.

Step #2: Decide on your "personal par" for each hole. They should all add up to a score of 89 or less. That's your blueprint for breaking 90. Now all that's left is to execute that plan.

Here are a few tips to help you execute your plan:

Tip #1: Warm-up before your round.
Stretch and stroke a few putts to get a feel for the speed of the greens. Hit some range balls. Getting loose before you hit your first tee shot can help get you off to a fast start that puts you in a positive frame of mind the entire round.

Tip #2: Play "within yourself." Play "smart."

Don't be a "hero." Don't over swing in an effort to hit the ball farther. Play the safe shot. Don't try shots you're not likely to execute. Avoid danger. Play away from hazards like water and sand traps.

Tip #3: Play one hole at a time.
You can't break 90 in one hole. And one bad hole won't kill you. Stay focused on your goal. You can make up a few strokes later in the round.

Tip #4: Play each hole backwards.
Before hitting your current shot, think about your next shot and where you'd like to hit it from. If you miss your first putt, leave it close enough to make the second-putt. If you're favorite distance is 120-yards and you're teeing off on a 350-yard hole, try to hit a 230-yard drive. Play away from hazards (trees, water, bunkers) on your approach shots to give yourself a better chance to chip on the green and two-putt for your "personal par."

The point is to think about your next shot before hitting your current shot. Then hit the shot that puts you in the best position to walk off the green with your "personal par."

Start playing "smart" golf and you'll increase your chances of breaking 90. And when you do, I want to hear about it. Send your success story to cs@getgolffit.com.

Good Luck!

Chapter 2 : Mastering the Basic Skills

The rest of this report is packed with information, tips, and strategies for breaking 90 consistently but it all builds on what we've already covered. So read all of it or pick and choose what you need. If you're weak spot is putting, study that section. If it's iron shots, I've got ideas to share for striking crisper iron shots.

Since we're playing the hole backwards let's start with…

How to 2-Putt Every Green…

What's the last shot of almost every hole?

A putt right? Unless you chip one in the hole or stuff your approach shot into the hole, your last shot on each hole will be a putt.

There are three kinds of putts:

1. A **"firm" putt**. This is a putt you expect to make – and you will make it most of the time. You stroke this putt confidently and aggressively. Your expectation is that after your stroke this putt, you'll reach down, pull your ball out of the cup, and move on to the next tee.

An example would be a tap-in from a few inches. You don't waste much time with the line and the speed, you just knock the ball into the hole with confidence. If you're going to break 90 consistently, you really should be confident that you'll make most puts of 3-feet or less.

2. A **"lag"** putt. The goal of a "lag" putt is to get the ball as close to the hole as possible so that the next putt is a tap-in. It's not an aggressive putt, you're just trying to putt the ball on the appropriate line with enough speed so that it stops close enough to the cup that you'll make the next putt. Preferably your putt will have enough speed to roll past the hole (that way you'll actually sink some of these "bombs" once in a while) but there's nothing catastrophic about leaving a "lag" putt a foot or two short because you can easily tap-in for a 2-putt. You don't expect to hole a "lag" putt although sometimes you will. And if you do, that's a bonus.

The distance of a "lag" putt could be different for different golfers but for someone who can't break 90 consistently (at least not yet!), the distance should be in the 15 to 20 foot range.

3. An **"intermediate"** putt. This is in between an "aggressive putt" and a "lag" putt. It's outside of your "circle of confidence" but it's inside "lag" putt range. The distance will generally be greater than 3 feet but less than 15 feet (or maybe a bit longer if you're a good putter).

This is similar to a "lag" putt but a bit more aggressive. Putts of this distance are definitely makeable so you should strive to NEVER leave an intermediate length putt short. You'll be amazed at how many of these putts you'll sink if you'll just get them to the hole!

If you're going to break 90 on a regular basis, you need to cut your 3-putts down to a minimum. Ideally you would eliminate 3-putts but even the pros 3-putt occasionally so it's not realistic to think you can completely eliminate the 3-putts.

A good goal that will go a long way to breaking 90 consistently is to have no more than 36 putts per round. That averages out to 2 putts per hole. So if you 3-putt once, you can make up for it with a one-putt.

You'd love to one-putt every green or even no-putt when you chip in. And you'll do that on occasion but let's focus on consistently 2-putting every green.

The first step in 2-putting every green is to make your second putt. Obvious, right? And here's how to do it consistently.

Remember, the "confident, aggressive "firm" putt I mentioned earlier? That's the type of putt you want for your second putt. That's the type of putt you're going to make most of the time. And if that's the type of putt you leave yourself with, you will 2-putt most greens.

The key is being "confident and aggressive" from as far away as possible. Everyone is confident they're going to make a one-inch putt or a six-inch putt or even a one-foot putt. Some golfers are still confident and aggressive from 2-feet whereas other golfers start shaking and getting nervous at that distance.

And when you're shaking and nervous standing over a putt, you can forget about making a confident, aggressive stroke.

So the key to 2-putting every green is to either:

1) stick your approach shot (or chip or pitch shot) so close to the pin that you're in confident, aggressive putting mode (and hopefully one-putt)

OR

2) "lag" your first putt into your "circle of confidence."

What's your "circle of confidence"? Here's an example. Let's say you're confident you'll sink putts of 3 feet or less most of the time. In that case you would imagine a 3-foot circle around the cup and that would be your "circle of confidence."

If you're confident putting from 4-feet and in, then your "circle of confidence" would be a 4-foot circle around the cup with the hole being in the middle. So golfers with confidence from longer distances have larger "circles of confidence."

And it logically follows that the larger your "circle of confidence" is, the more likely you are to 2-putt. So the first thing you must do is figure out the maximum distance from which you will make a confident and aggressive putting stroke and honestly expect to make the putt at least 80% of the time (that's 4 out of 5 times).

A good goal for a golfer with a handicap above 12 (and anyone who can't break 90 consistently has a handicap above 12) is to shoot for making any putt inside 3-feet 80% of the time.

A good way of hitting your "circle of confidence" is to dial in on the speed of the greens. After speaking to many PGA Pro's about why people have a tough time breaking 90, it usually comes back to putting... but specifically, distance control.

About 12 years ago, I was at Southern Hills with my girlfriend. We were both Nick Faldo fans and got there early to watch him warm up. The first thing he worked on was his putting. He didn't go to the range and bust balls.

Fanny tossed him a few balls and he dropped them at the edge of the green. He proceeded to hit a short putt (maybe 8 feet), a medium range putt to the exact center of the green, and then a long putt all the way to the edge of the green.

He picked up each ball and walked to the other side and repeated the process back to where he started.

Nick didn't stop here. He did the same thing from the ends of the green as well.

Of course, he went on to work on shorter putts through his routine... but, his first goal was to get a handle on the speed of the greens. Speed kills. Get the speed right, and you are certainly going to get your putts down.

But here's the bottom line: You have to make a decision. At what distance does your thought process change from one of supreme confidence ("I know I'm going to make this putt") to one of less confidence ("I just want to knock this one close so I can tap-in the next putt")?

Only you know the answer to that question. And if you don't know the answer, go to the putting green and figure it out. Stroke several one-foot putts, two-foot putts, and three-foot putts to figure out where your "circle of confidence" is.

Three feet is a reasonable goal, but if you're confident you're going to make 4-foot putts or 5-foot putts, then great! You're well on your way to breaking 90.

For arguments sake let's say you are confident and aggressive from 3 feet in. This means you pretty much ignore the break (unless it's more than a few inches) and confidently hole the putt most of the time.

Determining your "circle of confidence" is important because it dictates your "lag" putt. For example, if your first putt is 20-feet away, you're not realistically expecting to hole the putt. Your goal should be to putt the ball inside your "circle of confidence" for your second putt. If you're successful, you'll most likely make your second putt.

So in this example, with a 20-foot putt and your "circle of confidence" being 3-feet. Your goal would be to "lag" your first putt to within 3 feet of the hole. That would leave the ball inside your "circle of confidence."

In your mind, draw a circle with a 3-foot radius around the cup. Now "lag" your first putt so that it stops inside that circle. If you can do that, you'll most likely make the second putt because it's inside your 3-foot "circle of confidence."

Adjust this distance for your game. You ought to be confident you'll hole most putts from 3-feet or less. If not, then practice putting until you gain that confidence.

It's a fact that more strokes are lost on the putting green than anywhere else. Putting may not be the "sexy" part of the game but it's where you can lose a lot of strokes.

Now let's talk about intermediate putts....

Don't Leave Your Intermediate Putts Short!

Yogi Berra said it best: "*100% of short putts don't go in.*" There nothing more frustrating in the game of golf than stroking the almost perfect putt on the correct line – only to watch it come to a halt a few inches or a few revolutions short of the hole. Don't do it!!

What's the perfect speed? Putting guru Dave Pelz has done extensive research showing a putt that will roll 17 inches past the hole has the perfect speed. He's a former rocket scientist and he coaches Phil Mickelson so I'll just take his word for it.

Let's round that to 18 inches because that's a foot and half. What this means is that when you're putting add 18 inches to the putt. Stroke a 6 foot putt with enough speed to roll 7.5 feet. Stroke a 15-foot putt with enough speed to roll 16.5 feet.

This ensures that you won't leave the putt short and some of your putts will go in! And if you're 18-inches long, who cares? Anybody can make an 18-inch putt, right?

Of course, the farther away from the hole your first putt is, the more difficult to get the right speed. There will be a distance where you really just want to "lag" your first putt inside your "circle of confidence." But that distance is different for everyone.

You shouldn't be leaving 10-foot putts short. And you probably shouldn't be leaving 15-foot putts short either. These are the intermediate length putts I described earlier. An intermediate length putt is outside your "circle of confidence" but inside 15 or 20-feet depending on your putting skill.

You probably don't expect to hole intermediate length putts with any regularity but you still don't want to leave them short. You'll never make an intermediate putt if you leave it short. But if you hit it past the hole, it will drop in to the cup once in a while.

The distance of an intermediate length putt will be different for every golfer but a good length to use is 15feet. Don't leave putts of 15 feet or less short! You'll probably be surprised at how many you make when you get the ball to the hole!

But don't overdo it either. Remember, if you miss, you want the second putt to be inside your "circle of confidence" and the closer to the hole the better.
For intermediate length putts, cut your "circle of confidence" in half. I guess that makes it a "half-circle of confidence." Since you don't want to leave intermediate length putts short, eliminate the half of the "circle of confidence" that's short of the hole.

Focus on getting the ball to the hole and if you don't hole the putt, leaving it inside the "half-circle of confidence." That's the half of the "circle of confidence" behind the hole. If you leave it there, you haven't left the putt short and you've left yourself an easy second – putt that you're likely to make.

Developing this type of touch and feel requires practice. So practice your "firm" putts with the goal of making them. Practice your intermediate putts with the goal of not leaving them short but also stopping them inside your "half-circle of confidence."

And finally, there are "lag" putts. Again the distance where an intermediate putt turns into a "lag" putt will be different for various golfers but it's probably somewhere between 15 and 20 feet for a golfer who can't consistently break 90.

When you face a putt of 20-feet or longer, there's nothing disastrous about leaving your "lag" putt a foot or two short and tapping in for a two-putt.

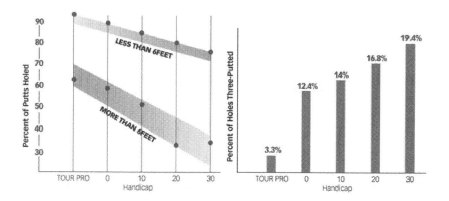

Putting Recap:

To break 90, the goal is to stroke 36 putts or less which means on average you will 2-putt each green. And in order to 2-putt most greens...

Step 1: Determine the radius of your "circle of confidence." It should be at least 3 feet. You should be confident that you'll make most of your putts from 3 feet or closer.

Step 2: When you're putting from outside your "circle of confidence," make sure you "lag" your first put into your "circle of confidence" to increase the chances that you'll hole your next putt and walk off the green having made 2-putts.

And finally, **don't leave intermediate putts short**.

You can't expect to make putts of 10 and 15 feet with regularity, but you won't make any of them if you leave them short. Stroke these "intermediate" putts with the speed to roll 17 inches past the cup. You'll be surprised at how many putts you make and if you miss, anyone can confidently hole a 17-inch putt.

Now that we're set on putting, let's move on.

Consistently Hitting the Green from 100 yards or less...

When you can hit your drives at least 200 yards and keep them in play and you can also hit a relatively straight second shot of 150 yards (and third shot on par 5 holes), you'll either reach the greens in regulation or you'll be within 100 yards of the green.

This is the "scoring zone." You'll take more shots inside 100 yards than you will outside 100 yards. Keeping those shots to a minimum increases your chances of breaking 90. And being able to consistently hit greens from 100 yards and closer will help tremendously.

Unlike "power" shots like driving the ball off the tee, these sorter shots are "finesse" shots. Accuracy is more important than distance here.

That means you don't need to aggressively attack the ball. You'll probably be more accurate if you take a more controlled swing giving up distance for accuracy.

Some golfers carry several wedges and have a different club for say a 60-yard shot, an 80-yard shot, and a 100-yard shot. That's fine. If you're comfortable with that then keep doing it.

When you go to the range, spend some time working on these shots and figure out the swing and the club that makes the ball go various distances from 20 to 100 yards. Pick a target (most practice ranges have yardage markers and target greens) and hit several shots until you're zoned in. That will give you much need confidence when you take your game to the course.

Another option is to use the same club and change your swing. For example, maybe you hit a soft pitching wedge 100 yards. That would be a full shot. Now you can take less than a full swing to hit the ball 80 yards, 60 yards, and 40 yards.

One way to accomplish this is to think of your swing like a clock. Think about a clock. "12 o'clock" would be when the golf club is straight up and down (just like the hands of a clock would be at 12 o'clock). A little less would be "11 o'clock," parallel to the ground (or perpendicular to your waist) would be "9 o'clock." And so on.

On your backswing, take your club back to "11 o'clock" and see how far it goes. Then "10 o'clock," and "9 o'clock". You'll quickly calibrate your swing to know how far the ball goes on your full swing, on your "10 o'clock" swing, etc.

Let's say your "10 o'clock" swing goes 60 yards. Now when you're on the course and you have a 60-yard pitch shot, you simply use your "10 o'clock" swing and you're on the green.

Practicing these shots and calibrating your golf swing to different distances from 100 yards and less will help your short game tremendously. And it will also go a long way towards achieving your goal of breaking 90 consistently.

There's actually no reason you can't use this same system for shots from 150 yards and in. Maybe you hit a 7-iron 150 yards. Then perhaps you hit a "soft" 7-iron (with a less aggressive, more controlled swing) 140-yards.

Now you can either hit a "hard" 8-iron or a "soft" 7-iron the next time you have a 140-yard shot. In any given situation, you may feel more comfortable hitting one shot rather than the other. It gives you more flexibility in your game.

The next skill you need to perfect is…

Consistently Hitting a Reasonably Straight 150-yard Iron Shot…

There's nothing magical about 150-yards. It's just a round number I picked but if you can hit a 200-yard drive followed by two 150-yard iron shots, then you can reach a 500-yard par 5 in three shots.

By "reasonably straight" I mean you don't need pinpoint accuracy. Most golfers naturally have either a natural draw (the ball moves from right to left for a right-handed golfer) or fade (the ball moves left to right for a right-handed golfer). And that's fine. Just play your natural shot.

It doesn't matter which iron you use either. The average golfer can hit a 7-iron 150 yards but if for you it's a 6-iron or a 5-iron, that's fine. And you're a longer hitter who hits an 8-iron 150 yards, that's fine too.

You could also use a hybrid club if you prefer. Hybrid clubs are great for new golfers and senior golfers. They can be easier to hit and you can get the ball in the air with slower swing speeds.

The club you use doesn't matter. What matters is that you can hit it consistently.

Another reason I chose 150 yards as the benchmark is that if you can hit a certain club 150 yards, then you can easily hit the ball 140 yards, 120 yards, 100 yards or less the less club and the same swing.

And that puts you in a great position to break 90 consistently.

If you can't consistently hit a fairly straight 150-yard iron shot (or hybrid), then work on developing that skill. Again, you could take a lesson or ask someone who's already mastered that skill for some tips.

Some golfers have trouble hitting their irons but it's really not that difficult. It's often because they don't understand the physics behind what puts the ball in the air.

Trust me, I'm no physicist, but this is not rocket science. Many golfers mistaken believe they must lift the ball into the air. And with that mistaken belief, they try to get under the ball and lift it into the air. This is called "scooping" and it's a great way to play bad golf.

Believe it or not, the exact opposite is true. Hitting down on the ball imparts spin on it that makes it rise up into the air – and with A LOT more force and power than when you "scoop" the ball.

Good golfers hit the ball first, before hitting the ground. That's why their divots start in front of the ball.

Understanding that simple concept and internalizing it is paramount to hitting crisp iron shots. Most high handicap golfers tend to hit their iron shots "fat." That means their golf club hits the ground before it hits the ball. That not only kills your club head speed but it makes the club bounce off the ground before it hits the ball.

Unfortunately I can't make you a better iron player in this short report. This is a blueprint for breaking 90 consistently – not a comprehensive golf instructional manual.
What I can say is that you'll probably find it helpful to find a "swing thought" that helps you hit better iron shots.

A common problem with high handicap golfers is that they swing "at" the ball. That causes tension in our grip right before impact and tension is the enemy of the golf swing. You should take a smooth swing like Ernie Els.

In other words, swing "through" the ball, not "at" the ball. Another way to say it is: "Take your practice swing and let the ball get in the way." Pretend the ball isn't even there. Just take a relaxed, tension-free swing as if the ball isn't even there.

Another tip that might help you hit more solid iron shots is to pick out a spot just in front of the ball and hit that spot. You could even put something small and flat like a penny in front of the ball and try to hit the penny.

This may seem or feel a bit strange at first – especially if you're a "scooper" or someone who tends to hit the ball "fat" – but focusing on a spot just in front of the ball promotes hitting the ball first with a downward strike. And you'll probably be AMAZED at how much farther the ball flies!

The next time you go to the practice range, work on striking your irons with a downward blow and hitting the ball before you hit the ground. You could start with half swings and work your way up to full swings if that helps.

When you understand and apply these simple concepts, you should easily be hitting your 7-iron 150 yards (or farther!).

Now let's move on to…

Consistently Hitting Your Drives 200 Yards or More (AND Keeping it in Play)…

Most golfers can hit their drives 200 yards. But consistently keeping it in play can be a challenge. If hitting fairways is a challenge for you, consider hitting less club off the tee.

There's no rule that says you have to hit your driver off the tee. And what good is it to hit a long drive, if you consistently miss the fairway and can't go for the green on your next shot?

The best golfers in the world understand this. Phil Mickelson won the 2013 British Open hitting a 3-wood off the tee. He took the driver out of his bag for the entire tournament.

Why would he do this?

He did it because he understands the importance of keeping the ball in play off the tee. It's no fun hitting second shots from deep grass and bad lies. Or worse, hitting third shots off the tee because you drove the first one out of bounds.

Tiger Woods won the 2006 British Open hitting irons off the tee. He only hit one driver the whole tournament. He wisely decided hitting irons off the tee to stay out of hazards gave him a better chance of winning than bombing his driver over the bunkers and hoping for the best.

If two of the best golfers of all-time are smart enough to leave their drivers in the bag and hit less club off the tee, then you should consider the same strategy – especially if you're consistently finding trouble off the tee.

I'm not saying you MUST hit less than driver off the tee – not at all. We're all different and maybe driving is your strength. Maybe you can consistently bomb your drives 250+ yards right down the middle of the fairway. If that's the case, then by all means, go ahead and hit your driver.

But if hitting a 3-wood, a 5-wood, a hybrid, or even a long iron off the tee keeps your tee shots in play more often and you can still hit it 200 yards or more, then give the shorter club a try for a round and see if you don't shoot a lower score.

If you can't hit the ball 200-yards off the tee, you need to create more swing speed. As I said earlier, this is NOT a book about the mechanics of the golf swing. It's all about helping you break 90 consistently.

But here are a few quick tips:

Swinging harder is usually NOT the answer. All kinds of bad things can happen when you over swing. Your mechanics break down and you start spraying the ball all over the course.

You increase your swing speed by increasing the strength of your core and by improving your flexibility. Your core is the collection of muscles and tendons between your thighs and your chest.

All other things being equal, a stronger core generates more swing speed. Core strength is like "golf horsepower" and just like a car with more horsepower goes faster, a player with more "golf horsepower" will have more swing speed and hit the ball farther.

Improving your flexibility will also increase your swing speed by increasing your range of motion. So work on increase the strength of your core and improving your flexibility.

You could practice swinging a weighted club or swinging two clubs at the same time.

In fact, EVERY golf fitness program I design for you has Range of Motion as well as flexibility designed in. You also get my Pre-Round Warm Up that I receive so much positive feedback from. To tide you over though, here are a few ROM (Range of Motion) drills you can use.

Egyptian
1. Start with arms out straight and your palms facing down.
2. Pivot and turn to one side while keeping your arms in the same spot in space.
3. Both hands should turn up as much as possible.
4. Switch sides keeping your shoulders in line.

Arm Circles

1. Draw maximal circles with one or both arms.

2. Repeat in opposite direction.

Get **Golf Fit**.com

Hula Hoop

1. Imitate a hoola hoop motion.
2. Keep shoulders stationary and make big circles with your hips.

If distance is not a problem, but hitting fairways is…you might consider taking a lesson. Or if you want a free lesson, ask someone who's better than you for help. Ask someone who hits their driver long and straight to watch your swing and point out what you need to correct. It's often something simple. But there are way too many swing flaws to cover in this short report.

If you do seek free advice, be careful who you ask. Take advice only from golfers who can hit their drives long and straight. In other words, seek help from golfers who have already mastered the skill you're working to develop.

And that's it! When you master these four basic skills:

✓ consistently driving the ball 200 yards or more (and keeping it in play)
✓ consistently hitting your second shots 150 yards or more (and your third shot on par 5s)

✓ consistently hitting greens from 100 yards or less, and

✓ consistently 2-putt most greens

and use the proven blueprint for breaking 90, you should be shooting in the 80's consistently and having more fun playing golf.

Helpful Resources:

Core to Score: http://getgolffit.com/core-to-score

A Swing for Life: Revised and Revisited: http://amzn.com/1451676530

Get Golf Fit on Facebook: https://www.facebook.com/getfitforgolf

And if you're not already receiving weekly tips from the blog, sign up here: http:www.getgolffit.com

Other Books by Christian Henning:

Golf Fitness: Shed Pounds to Shave Strokes

Shed Pounds to Shave Strokes utilizes 'Turbulence Training' and 'Translation Training' to keep your body in an ever adapting state. Through forced adaptation, we force the body to burn fat and improve golf performance. The program uses both weight training and short-burst cardio sessions.

LOWER YOUR SCORE WHILE BURNING FAT & BUILDING STAMINA

Professional trainer and golfer, Christian Henning has designed a golf specific workout to give you the golf body you dream about.

Get Your Copy Here: ==> http://golff.it/shed

- Melt Fat and Lower Your Score with golf specific workouts!
- Dumbbells, Stability Ball, and a Chair are all you need.
- Beginner, Intermediate, and Advanced Workouts included.
- Email Support from Golf Fitness Specialists.
- Download Now, Workout Today!

Golf Fitness: 30 Yards or More in 30 Days or Less

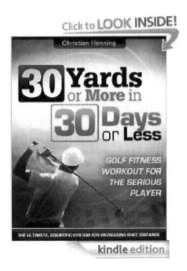

30 Yards or More in 30 Days or Less is the workout to do AFTER Shed Pounds to Shave Strokes. This more advanced program to begin immediately after Shed Pounds is our core strengthening and power workout program.

This 4-week (advanced) to 8-week (Intermediate and beginner) workout program is designed to build on the base you create in Shed Pounds to Shave Strokes. In a nutshell, this is a tour pro caliber workout designed to improve golf performance and provide you with more distance, stamina, and control.

ADD DISTANCE THROUGH STRENGTH & FLEXIBILITY

Professional trainer and golfer, Christian Henning has designed a golf specific workout to give you the golf body you dream about.

Get Your Copy Here: ==> http://golff.it/30in30

- Build Balance, Flexibility, Strength, and Power in just 30 days
- Dumbbells, Stability Ball, and a Chair are all you need.
- Beginner, Intermediate, and Advanced Workouts included.
- Email Support from Golf Fitness Specialists.
- Download Now, Workout Today!

My Mission

To help 1 million golfers by the year 2020 to improve their health and play the greatest game of them all longer.

Aid in eliminating pain and injuries, improve their golf game through improved performance and consistency, and live longer so they can comfortably play golf in to their golden years.

What has inspired me to help 1 million men and women transform their lives?

Like many Americans, bad health has taken many loved ones way to early that were close to me. Both my mother and father died in their early 60's.

Smokers… who regularly ate fast food.. and cooked dinners using a deep fryer… and rarely exercised.

Even my grandfather passed away too soon in his early 70's.

Growing up, Thursday was when my dad, grandfather and I would go play golf together. My dad was decent and could hit the ball a long way.. my grandfather was like Yoda with a sand iron. He was even short like Yoda. :)

The matches were competitive but most of all - fun.

I'll never forget those days and I wish they could have gone on forever. The matches ended before they had to. Bad health took my two favorite golfing buddies from me.

Sad – and preventable, to a point.

We all die some day. However, you can extend your life by adopting some daily rituals.. Rituals that take a small fraction of time each day… but lend years to the end of your life. I'm a firm believer that taking care of yourself all of your life will help you age gracefully in your golden years. Mom, dad, and my grandpa didn't take care of themselves as well as they could have.

Who knows how many years we lost together due to the bad choices they made concerning food and exercise?

I was alone.

No one close enough to me to ask for advice when I needed a fathers advice.. or a grandfathers.. or a mothers. No one to see the accomplishments I would rise to. No one to help when the days were dark.

Yes, It Can Happen To Anyone…

Most of my life I have been physically active and taken reasonable care of myself – however – I did go through a five year span in a corporate environment where I literally 'let myself go'. Soon after my mom passed away I quit my job as an assistant pro at a golf course.. to get a real job.

I had a child on the way and could no longer get by "having fun" on the golf course. Within a few years in the corporate world I discovered I was on the same path as my parents. Bad habits soon developed as I tried to fit in to the corporate culture.

My weight ballooned up to 245 pounds. Prior to the corporate job, my weight fluctuated between 195 and 205 pounds.

Gone were the days of golfing from morning to night and being physically active. My new destiny appeared to be a wobbly chair under fluorescent lighting. I was miserable not only physically, but mentally.

I hated my situation. Kept away from the game I loved so much and trapped in an office...

Days and weeks went by without touching a golf club. My 'touch' soon followed and I became scared to even play a round of golf. If I did play, I knew the result would be depressing. Invited to play golf with friends, I would always decline. Embarrassed of how I looked and how far I had fallen athletically.

Going from a scratch golfer to someone who couldn't break 90 was a tough pill to swallow.

Even more difficult was the image I would see in the mirror. My muscular body shrouded with pounds of unwanted fat. Muscles that had lost their tone and disappeared. A few years after working in misery, I decided to finally play golf with some of my co-workers and realized my distance and my game were totally gone. I used to CRUSH the ball and out-drive just about anyone.

No longer.

I went back home.. embarrassed and ashamed.

How could I let myself go this far? I had gained 45 pounds of pure lard! I could barely walk up a flight of stairs without getting out of breath. My eating habits were relegated to drive-through windows and fast food establishments. My job was unfulfilling.

Ridiculous!

One day, I decided enough was enough. I was first going to get back my health, and second, get back my golf game. The third step would be to regain financial control of my situation.

Let me tell you, it was tough. Mentally it was as hard as anything I have ever done.

It took five years of dedicated effort to reverse the five years of 'lardiness' (my word for laziness and adding poundage).

Five years to build my lardiness, five years to take it off.

Think about that for a second… five years… Please understand this process can take awhile. Losing that fat and regaining my game were worth the five years of effort.

Maybe the weight loss was a bit slow and it didn't melt off like it does with some folks.. but I gained experience and knowledge that help me connect with people who are like I was... people that need my help.

I learned that playing golf and fitness both made me happy. Once my health was back, my golf game was in check. My joy for the game increased.

My distance was back, albeit with a new twist – I could hit it even further! In addition, my self confidence surged. I felt great about who I was and how I arrived there.

Along my journey I became a certified personal trainer, read countless books and journals, and watched tons of DVD's. And what about the job I hated? I quit and started three businesses I own, of which I still run two today. Five short years I transformed my entire life from the inside out.

Golf, fitness, and running my own businesses are my daily rituals now.

The inspiration to help 1 million women and men to transform their lives is simple... it's about helping others spend Thursday afternoon with their father and grandfather.

Legal Disclaimer

You must get your physician's approval before beginning this exercise program. These recommendations are not medical guidelines but are for educational purposes only. You must consult your physician prior to starting this program or if you have any medical condition or injury that contraindicates physical activity. This program is designed for healthy individuals 18 years and older only.

The information in this report is meant to supplement, not replace, proper exercise training. All forms of exercise pose some inherent risks. The editors and publishers advise readers to take full responsibility for their safety and know their limits. Before practicing the exercises in this book, be sure that your equipment is maintained, and do not take risks beyond your level of experience, aptitude, training and fitness. The exercises and dietary programs in this book are not intended as a substitute for any exercise routine or treatment or dietary regimen that may have been prescribed by your physician.

Don't lift heavy weights if you are alone, inexperienced, injured, or fatigued. Don't perform any exercise unless you have been shown the proper technique by a certified personal trainer or certified strength and conditioning specialist. Always ask for instruction and assistance when lifting. Don't perform any exercise without proper instruction. Always do a warm-up prior to strength training and interval training.

See your physician before starting any exercise or nutrition program. If you are taking any medications, you must talk to your physician before starting any exercise program, including Core 2 Score, Shed Pounds to Shave Strokes or 30 Yards or More in 30 Days or Less. If you experience any lightheadedness, dizziness, or shortness of breath while exercising, stop the movement and consult a physician.

You must have a complete physical examination if you are sedentary, if you have high cholesterol, high blood pressure, or diabetes, if you are overweight, or if you are over 30 years old. Please discuss all nutritional changes with your physician or a registered dietician. If your physician recommends that you don't use Golf Fitness: Core 2 Score, please follow your doctor's orders.

41256645R00033

Made in the USA
San Bernardino, CA
10 November 2016